ABCDEF
GHIJKLMN
OPQRSTUV
WXYZ!!

ABCDEF
GHIJKLMN
OPQRSTUV
WXYZ!!

THE ABCs OF ROCK

THE ABCs OF ROCK

BY MELISSA DUKE MOONEY

ILLUSTRATIONS BY PRINT MAFIA

TRICYCLE PRESS
Berkeley

All rights reserved. Published in the United States by Tricycle Press, an imprint of Random House Children's Books,
a division of Random House, Inc., New York.
www.randomhouse.com/kids

Tricycle Press and the Tricycle Press colophon are registered trademarks of Random House, Inc.

Special thanks to Annissa Mason and Skip Rudsenske for their tireless efforts in bringing this book to fruition and to
Marc Geiger for his valuable help in securing licenses. You guys "rock!"

Library of Congress Cataloging-in-Publication Data

Mooney, Melissa Duke.
  The ABCs of rock / Melissa Duke Mooney and Print Mafia.
      p. cm.
  Includes bibliographical references and index.
1. Rock musicians—Biography—Juvenile literature. I. Print Mafia. II.
Title.
  ML3929.M65 2009
  781.66092'2—dc22
  [B]
                              2008053139

ISBN 978-1-58246-293-6 (hardcover)
ISBN 978-1-58246-357-5 (Gibraltar lib. bdg.)
Printed in China

Design by Toni Tajima
Typeset in Boycott, Helvetica Neue, Flyswim, Stamp Gothic
The illustrations in this book were created digitally.

1 2 3 4 5 6 – 15 14 13 12 11 10

First Edition

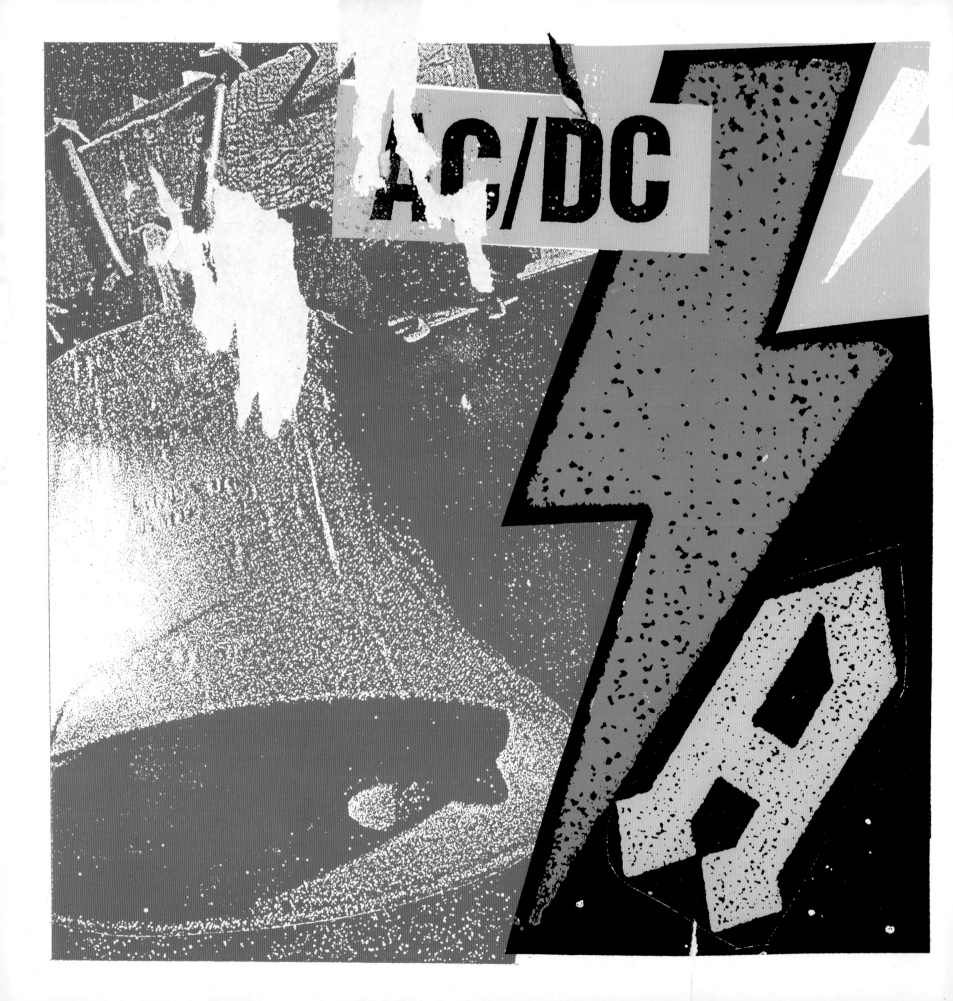

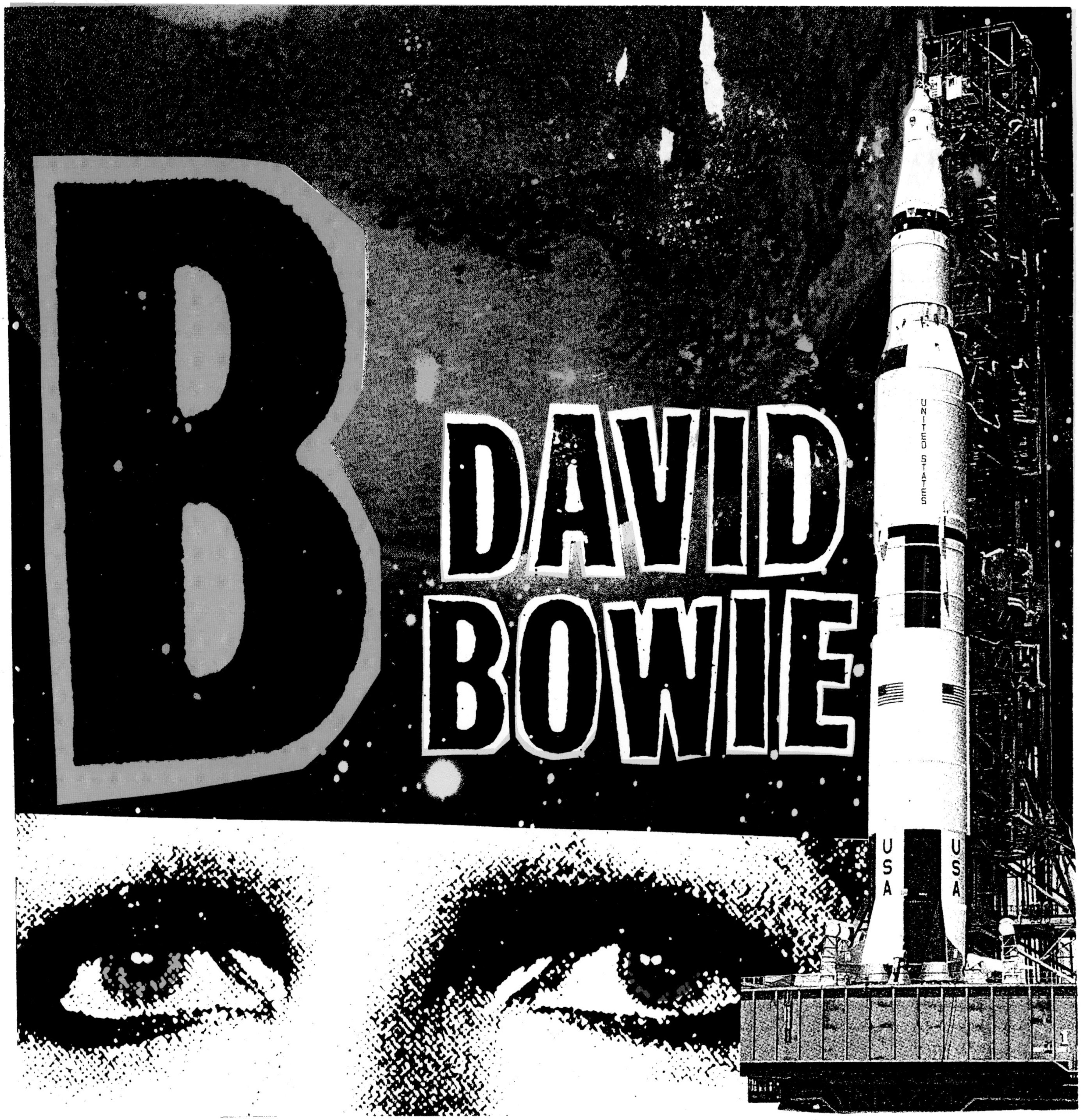
B
DAVID
BOWIE
UNITED STATES
USA
USA

THE CLASH

ELVIS
COSTELLO

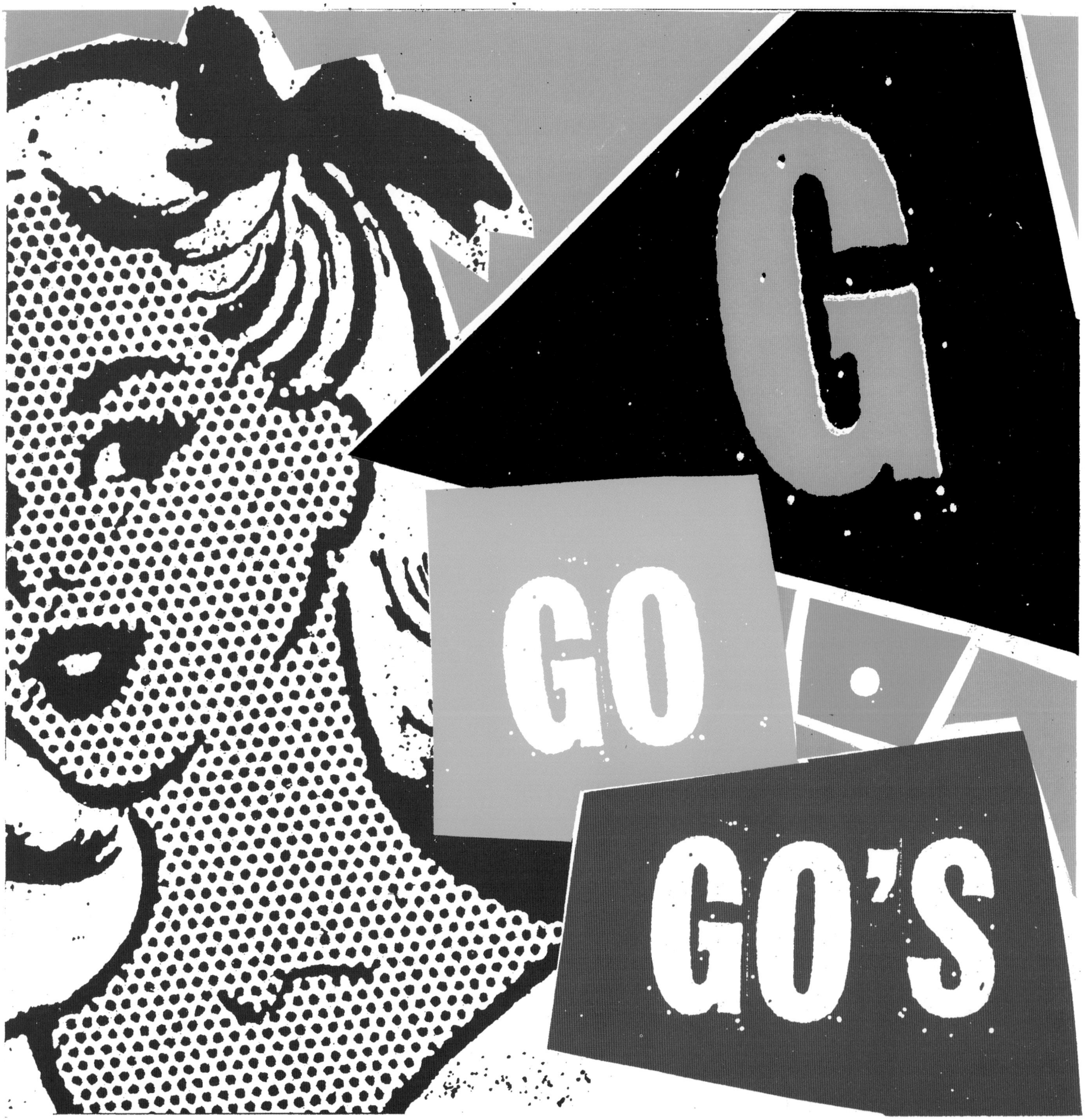
G
GO
GO'S

HEART

H

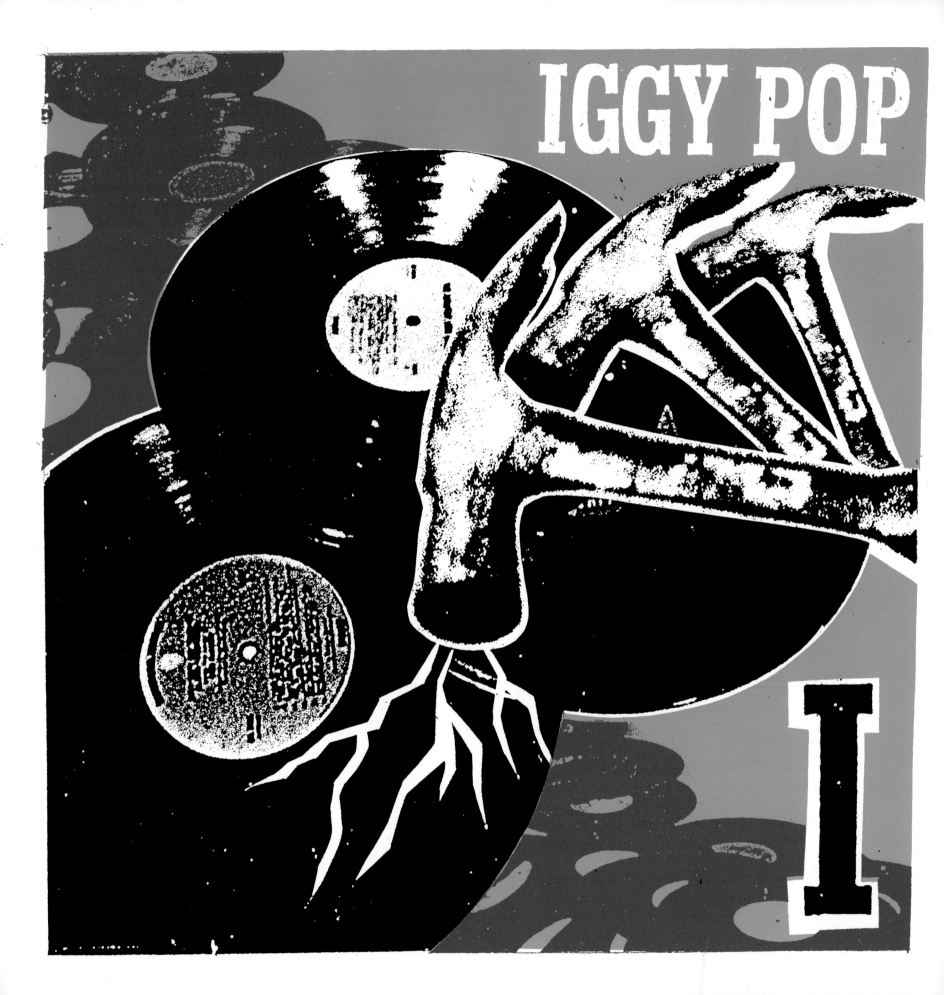

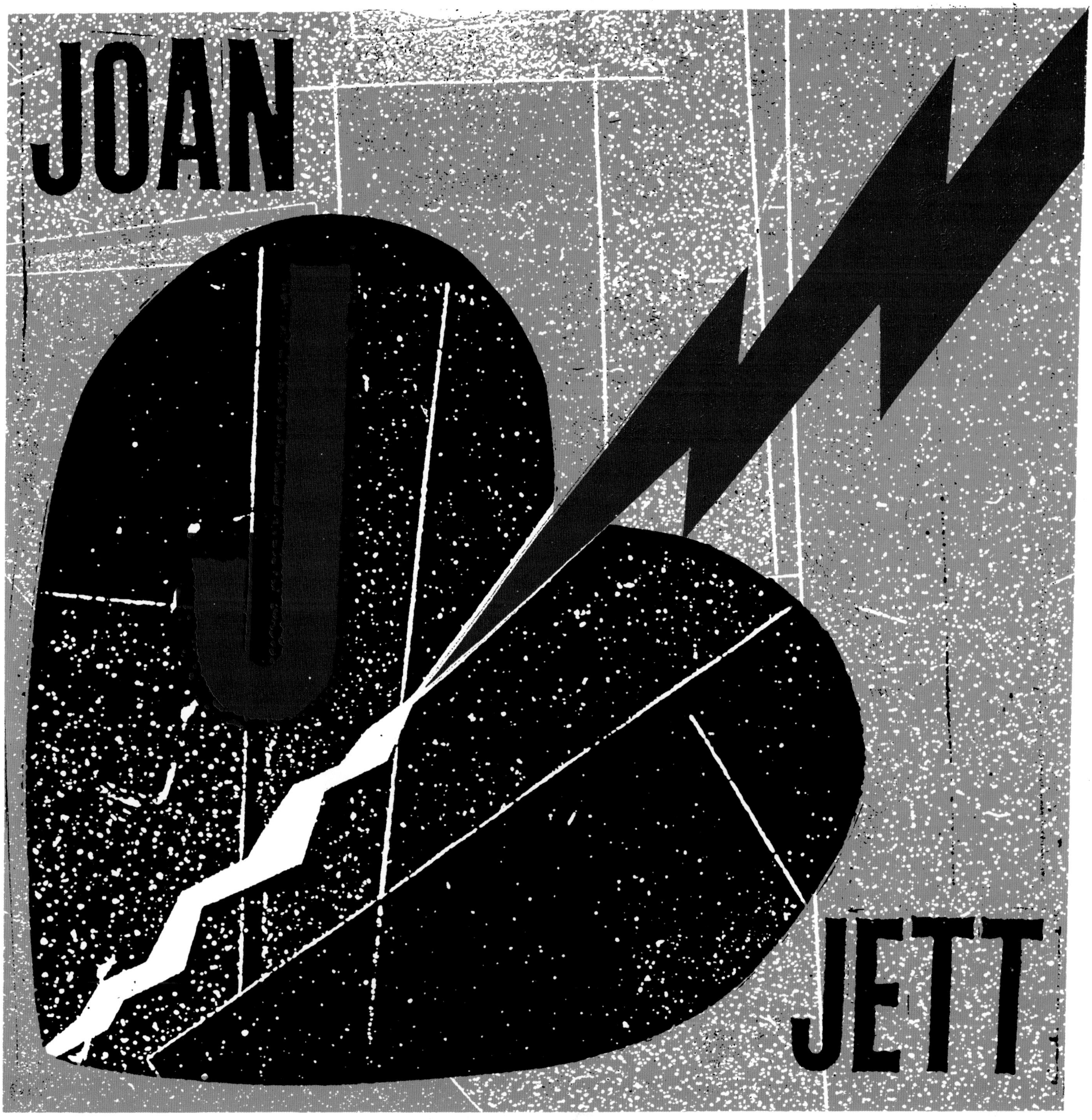
JOAN
J
JETT

THE POLICE

S

SONIC YOUTH

THE VELVET UNDERGROUND

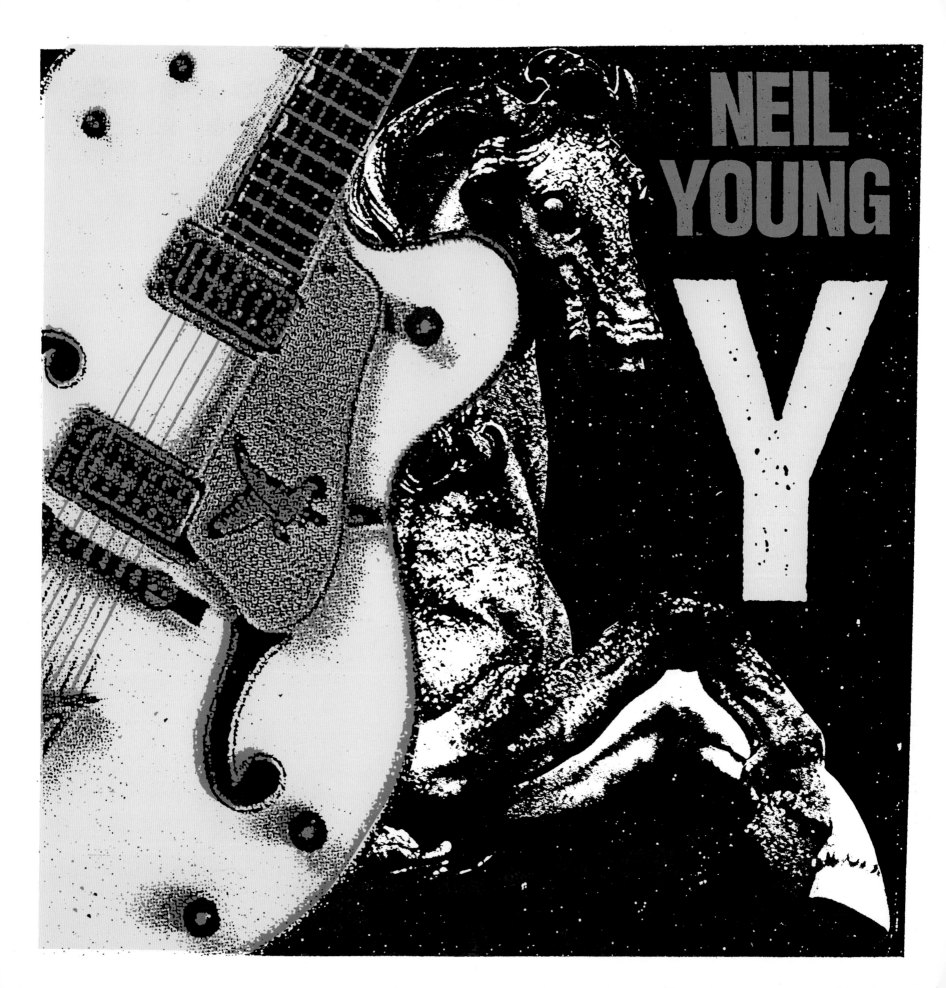

ART NOTES BY PRINT MAFIA CO-CREATORS JIM MADISON AND CONNIE COLLINGSWORTH

AC/DC: This band is one of our favorites and probably the first hard rock band that Connie ever listened to, courtesy of riding around in the back of her older sister's Pontiac Trans Am in the midseventies. She loved the band's eight-track album covers and the crunch of Angus' guitar. The AC/DC logo and lightning bolt are as iconic as they come.

DAVID BOWIE: This image pays tribute to our favorite Bowie song, "Space Oddity." The song is an atmospheric journey through time, space, and rock mythology.

THE CLASH: It was difficult to compete with all of The Clash's amazing artwork. They are the very definition of punk. We attempted to create what could have been a seven-inch vinyl cover for "The Only Band That Matters."

BOB DYLAN: Bob Dylan has had such an incredible, multi-decade-spanning career that it was difficult to pin down what era or look to go with. We finally chose his transition out of the folk acoustic era and his decision to "go electric" in the midsixties.

ELVIS COSTELLO: Melissa was a big fan of Elvis Costello so the choice for "E" was obvious. To us, Elvis Costello embodies the look and sound of new wave/punk. We wanted to create our version of an early eighties Elvis Costello album cover or T-shirt.

FLEETWOOD MAC: We could have chosen the more popular *Rumours*-era Fleetwood Mac but felt that the *Rumours* album cover already said it all. Connie has been a huge Fleetwood Mac fan since her teenage years and wanted to try to capture the spirit of *Tusk,* an album that, to us, sounds wild, out of control, and experimental.

GO-GO'S: The Go-Go's roots are in LA's early eighties punk scene. If you listen to the male-dominated bands coming out of there at that time, Hollywood seems to be a hard, gritty, violent place. The Go-Go's were able to embody punk's ethic and musical integrity, but their sound was a mixture of punk and pure pop gold. Like the bright-eyed, Lichtenstein blonde of our image, their music hints at a carefree, fun-in-the-sun lifestyle that can be found just on the other side of the Hollywood sign.

HEART: One of the great things about the Wilson sisters' music—besides Ann's stunning voice and Nancy's epic guitar sound—is that it gives us heavy rock'n'roll from a female point of view. We tried to work that hard-edged femininity into a play on the title of their classic album, *Dog and Butterfly.*

IGGY POP: Iggy is The Godfather of Punk Rock. We wanted to show the aggression and energy that is Iggy Pop music.

JOAN JETT: Joan Jett embodies rock'n'roll: her look, her sound, her attitude. She should be recognized as one of the great rock'n'roller's of our time, male or female. We tried to portray the hard crunch of Joan's pure rock sound and combine it with the heart that she puts into everything she does.

KISS: Both of us are huge KISS fans and have been since childhood. We don't remember a time when we weren't aware of KISS. Once we saw that makeup, we were hooked.

LED ZEPPELIN: They are a powerful rock band, but what attracts us most to Zeppelin's music is its beauty and mysticism. Like a zeppelin floating over a concrete city, the light and the heavy are both present in their music.

BOB MARLEY: We really wanted to include reggae music in the book. It has influenced so many rock bands, and Bob Marley was its greatest ambassador. Marley's music has such forceful messages and yet its sounds are so gentle and joyous—we felt a lion captured it perfectly.

NIRVANA: We were the same age and came from a similar social and economic upbringing as Kurt, Krist, and Dave. When they made it big, it made us feel that we could create art our way, too. We wanted to include Nirvana because they changed the direction of rock. Nirvana first came on the scene at a time when music on the radio had become glossy and fake—boy bands, pop princesses, and people lip-synching to studio singers' prerecorded tracks. Nirvana were real. This is our tribute to "Smells Like Teen Spirit."

OZZY OSBOURNE: Jim's first concert ever was Ozzy's Bark at the Moon tour. He was blown away by the theatrics of the show. To him, Ozzy seemed larger than life. We wanted the art to reflect Ozzy's dark and powerful stage persona.

THE POLICE: The Police have a huge number of instantly recognizable songs full of memorable, haunting lyrics. For this image, we wanted to combine the imagery and colors of *Synchronicity* with the watching eyes of "Every Breath You Take."

QUEEN: Freddie Mercury had one of the most recognizable and beautiful voices in rock. When we think of Queen, we think of the band's grand, almost majestic, presence and sound. The name suits them perfectly.

R.E.M.: To us, R.E.M. are the founding fathers of alternative music. They have outlasted most of their contemporaries and have continued to evolve and still maintain that integrity that drew us to them in high school and college. Here, we pay tribute to the great song that is "Man on the Moon."

SONIC YOUTH: For Sonic Youth, we tried to create an image that would evoke the band's distorted sound, which to us is a combination of fuzz, noise, and crunch.

TALKING HEADS: Talking Heads create what we call "thoughtful music": smart compositions with beautiful melodies to draw you in. They embody the New York underground scene. We wanted to be quite literal with our interpretation of a "talking head" because we think it is one of the great band names in rock'n'roll.

U2: What can you say about U2? They have the blueprint down for longevity in rock'n'roll: they keep their music and image relevant and constantly reinvent themselves. We have been fans since high school and love the early albums, but chose to focus on a later band image: Zoo TV.

THE VELVET UNDERGROUND: The Velvet Underground were the house band for Andy Warhol and his New York-based Factory. In the sixties, photography became the dominant art form for advertising and the promotion of pop icons—two things that preoccupied the artists of the Factory. Andy Warhol's iconic silkscreen prints were the inspiration behind this piece.

THE WHITE STRIPES: While relative newcomers to the rock scene, The White Stripes are already classic. They are current yet embrace the past, and their influence will be heard in the music of our children's children. We chose to depict their love and support of vinyl records.

X: X are LA punk. Their music and style give you a glimpse of the other side of LA—that place far away from Disneyland and sunny beaches. Their music evokes the sweaty clubs, the neon lights, and the punk lifestyle of a Hollywood that has nothing to do with glitz and glamour.

NEIL YOUNG: Neil Young is a living legend. His haunting voice, the atmospheric guitar, the thoughtful and timeless lyrics—all of these combine to make his music incredibly compelling. We also wanted to evoke the rustic imagery and sense of freedom in his lyrics through the use of Old West colors.

ZZ TOP: Jim says that whenever he hears any ZZ Top song, he pictures Ford's Eliminator coupe hot rod. That car is an inescapable part of their image.

ABCDEF
GHIJKLMN
OPQRSTUV
WXYZ!

ABCDEF
GHIJKLMN
OPQRSTUV
WXYZ!!